SPOTLIGHT ON NATURE
PANDA

MELISSA GISH

CREATIVE EDUCATION · CREATIVE PAPERBACKS

Published by Creative Education and Creative Paperbacks
P.O. Box 227, Mankato, Minnesota 56002
Creative Education and Creative Paperbacks are imprints
of The Creative Company
www.thecreativecompany.us

Design and production
by Chelsey Luther
Art direction by Rita Marshall
Printed in the United States of America

Photographs by Alamy (Arterra Picture Library, BIOSPHOTO, Andrea
Izzotti, National Geographic Image Collection, Trinity Mirror/Mirrorpix, Xin-
hua, Xue Yubin/Xinhua/Alamy Live News, Zhang Bowen/Xinhua/Alamy Live
News, Zou Zheng/Xinhua/Alamy Live News), Dreamstime (Isselee, Venus
Kaewyoo, Luceluceluce), Getty Images (Nada Pecnik/Visuals Unlimited,
MOHD RASFAN/Stringer/AFP, GUILLAUME SOUVANT/AFP, VCG/
Visual China Group), iStockphoto (Hung_Chung_Chih, powerofforever),
Minden Pictures (Katherine Feng), Shutterstock (HoyaBouquet,
Eric Isselee, Sudowoodo)

Library of Congress Cataloging-in-Publication Data
Names: Gish, Melissa, author.
Title: Panda / Melissa Gish.
Series: Spotlight on nature.
Includes index.
Summary: A detailed chronology of developmental milestones drives this life
study of pandas, including their habitats, physical features, and conservation
measures taken to protect these black-and-white bears.
Identifiers: LCCN 2018041321 / ISBN 978-1-64026-183-9 (hardcover)
/ ISBN 978-1-62832-746-5 (pbk) / ISBN 978-1-64000-301-9 (eBook)
Subjects: LCSH: Giant panda—China—Sichuan Sheng—Juvenile literature. /
Bears—China.
Classification: LCC QL737.C27 G528 2019 / DDC 599.7890951/38—
dc23

First Edition HC 9 8 7 6 5 4 3 2 1
First Edition PBK 9 8 7 6 5 4 3 2 1

CONTENTS

GIANT PANDAS

of the Qionglai Mountains

In the lower reaches of the Qionglai (*CHONG-lie*) Mountains in southwestern China, a dense bamboo forest grows in the understory of towering dawn redwood, Chinese cedar, and larch. Massive takins, tufted deer, and tiny Indian muntjacs browse for tender vegetation. Spotted linsangs scurry through fallen leaves hunting mice, while stump-tailed macaques chatter in the treetops. Sitting with hind legs splayed, leaning against a likiang spruce, a female giant panda munches a stalk of bamboo.

It is mid-August and about 70 °F (21.1 °C) in the montane forest. A light mist hangs in the air, leaving tiny droplets of moisture on the panda's thick fur. For nearly five months, a baby panda has been developing inside the female panda's body. She has been eating steadily for days, knowing she will have to forgo food and water for up to a week when her baby arrives—which will be very soon.

CLOSE-UP
Natural raincoats

A panda's coat has two layers. The outer layer is long and coarse. Beneath this is a dense, woolly layer. Panda fur is slightly oily, which prevents water from soaking the animal's skin.

CHAPTER ONE

LIFE BEGINS

The giant panda is a bear species that is found only in scattered forests of China's Qinling (*CHIN-ling*), Minshan, Qionglai, Daxiangling (*DA-see-YUNG-leeng*), Xiaoxiangling (*shee-OW-shee-OWNG-ling*), and Liangshan (*LYUNG-shan*) Mountains. Fewer than 1,900 pandas exist in the wild. In the 1980s, scientists discovered a unique panda in an isolated area of the Qinling Mountains, in the southern Shaanxi (*SHAH-ahn-SEE*) Province. Called the Qinling panda, this giant panda has brown fur instead of black like other pandas. Scientists believe that inbreeding could be the cause of this mutation. In 2005, the Qinling panda was recognized as an official subspecies. Since its discovery, it has been spotted fewer than 10 times.

QIONGLAI MOUNTAIN GIANT PANDA MILESTONES

DAY (1)

» Born
» Pink-skinned with sparse, wispy white hair
» Weight: 4 ounces (113 g)
» Length: 7 inches (17.8 cm)

CLOSE-UP
Panda potty

A newborn cub's muscles are so weak that it cannot urinate or defecate on its own. After feeding her cub, a mother panda licks her cub's belly to help it pass waste.

— FEATURED FAMILY —

Welcome to the World

In a forested valley of the Qionglai Mountains, the female giant panda has made a den in the shelter of a rock pile. She has covered the floor with leafy bamboo and twigs. Outside, light rain falls, but inside, it is warm and dry. The panda feels a stirring inside her body. She sits up, leaning her back against the den wall. Within just a few minutes, her baby has been born. She gently grasps the tiny baby in her jaws. She lays the cub against her chest and begins to lick it clean.

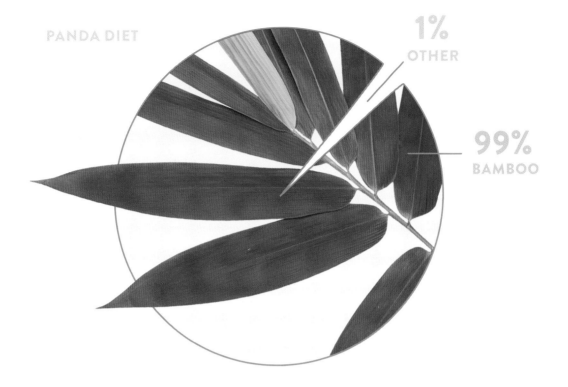

PANDA DIET

1%
OTHER

99%
BAMBOO

Like all bears, giant pandas are omnivores, which means they eat both meat and plants. They have sharp teeth and powerful jaws. But unlike their relatives, pandas eat mostly plants. They may occasionally eat a bamboo rat or a baby bird that has fallen from its nest, but about 99 percent of their diet is made up of bamboo. They must consume a lot—up to 80 pounds (36.3 kg) every day—to get enough nutrients. While pandas have no trouble grinding bamboo to a pulp with their broad molars, they prefer to feed on the more tender shoots and leaves. Pandas may also snack on flowers, vines, and other grasses. More than half of every day is spent eating.

(3) WEEKS

Black hair begins to grow
Calls to mother frequently
Weight: 1.3 pounds (0.6 kg)

About half of all panda births result in twins. Because the father panda leaves after mating, a mother panda must care for her offspring alone. She cannot feed two babies, called cubs, at the same time. She must choose which cub to care for. A newborn panda is nearly 1,000 times smaller than its mother. It is completely helpless. It can neither see nor hear. From nose to rump, the cub is only as long as a stick of butter. A mother panda holds her cub close to her chest to keep it warm. She feeds it milk from her body. Cubs cry out for milk about every two hours.

CLOSE-UP
Eating bamboo

Pandas break bamboo stalks into pieces 10 to 16 inches (25.4–40.6 cm) long. Then they strip off the hard bark to get at the soft inside. They can devour a piece in about 40 seconds. Panda throats have a special lining that protects against splinters.

FEATURED FAMILY

First Meal

As a newborn, the panda cub's immune system is not yet working. Without this, the cub could easily get sick and die. But he is protected by his mother's milk. In addition to important nutrients, the milk contains a substance called colostrum. It works like medicine to keep the cub healthy. After 30 to 40 days, the cub's own immune system will work. The colostrum will disappear from his mother's milk.

A NEWBORN

panda is nearly

1,000 TIMES

than its mother.

⑥ **WEEKS**

- ▸ Eyes open partially
- ▸ Calls less frequently
- ▸ Weight: 2.5 pounds (1.1 kg)

CLOSE-UP
Communicating with cubs

In 2015, research from China showed that pandas have a language of sorts. A cub makes a squeaky *gee-gee* to say, "I'm hungry," and *wow-wow* to say, "I'm unhappy." Mothers may respond with a sheeplike *bah* to say, "Okay." A birdlike *wheet* means, "You're driving me nuts!"

CHAPTER TWO

EARLY ADVENTURES

Adult giant pandas have few natural enemies. Wild dogs called dholes (*DOLZ*) may attack pandas, but these animals are endangered and rarely cross paths with pandas anymore. Small cubs may be snatched by jackals, yellow-throated martens, and snow leopards. Mothers must be vigilant. For the first three months of a cub's life, its mother will spend about 80 percent of her time just holding it. When she leaves the cub to forage for food, it will be for only very short periods of time. For a young cub, the challenges are staying safe and warm, getting enough to eat, and not getting accidentally crushed by its mother—it's rare, but it happens.

(8) WEEKS

- Eyes fully open
- Begins to crawl
- Ceases calling, since he can see mother
- Weight: 4 pounds (1.8 kg)

Adult pandas vocalize very little for the most part, but cubs are quite noisy, crying and squealing when they are hungry or cold. First-time mothers sometimes drop their cubs. It takes practice to become skilled at lifting and carrying them. Once cubs are able to walk, they become highly active. But they do not stray from their mother's side. They playfully clamber over her, practice climbing on stumps and rocks, and run and roll around. As adults, pandas do not run—they just walk quickly.

CLOSE-UP
Stomach helpers

Bamboo is difficult to digest. Tiny organisms called microbes living in pandas' stomachs help break down bamboo. The microbes continue to live in panda dung, so young cubs sometimes eat their mothers' dung to get extra microbes.

—————— FEATURED FAMILY ——————

Look Who's Walking

The Qionglai giant panda cub is now three months old. His mother has been away from the den for a few hours, foraging in the forest. The cub has been sleeping. When she returns, the mother flops down on the floor of the den. She lies on her side and reaches her paw out toward the cub. He gets to his feet and takes a few steps toward her, cautiously finding his footing among the leaves and twigs. His mother calls softly to him as he comes closer. His steps are slow and mindful today, but within another week or two, he will be bounding around the den with carefree excitement.

Cubs are quite noisy, CRYING AND SQUEALING when they are HUNGRY OR COLD

 WEEKS

> Stands and walks a few steps
> Coat is thick and fluffy
> Weight: 7.5 pounds (3.4 kg)
> Length: 20 inches (50.8 cm)

FEATURED  FAMILY

Give It a Try

The cub's mother is sleepy, but the cub is wide awake. He is now strong enough to climb onto his mother by himself. While she rests, the cub fills his tummy with milk. After his meal, he slides down his mother's belly and tumbles to the ground. He jumps to his feet, gingerly grasps his mother's ear between his teeth, and gives it a gentle tug. Then he climbs over her face, jumps on her belly, and slides down again. This play helps strengthen the cub's muscles.

PLAY
helps **strengthen** the cub's
MUSCLES.

(4) MONTHS

- Runs short distances around mother
- About half a set of baby teeth
- Weight: 20 pounds (9.1 kg)

CLOSE-UP
Panda poo

Pandas digest and use only about 17 percent of the bamboo they eat, which leaves their dung bright green. Throughout the day, a panda passes dung up to 100 times—even while napping. Pandas pass 40 to 60 pounds (18.1–27.2 kg) of dung every day.

CHAPTER THREE
LIFE LESSONS

When a panda cub is six to seven months old, its mother will lead it out of the den to explore the forest. The cub gets its first tastes of water and bamboo. Under its bark, bamboo has a texture similar to asparagus and a lightly sweet flavor that is similar to corn. Pandas can eat about 25 of the more than 1,300 different bamboo species. However, they usually stick to four or five kinds that contain a variety of vitamins and minerals. While bamboo contains moisture, it does not have enough to sustain adult pandas. A daily intake of fresh water is vital to pandas' survival. Pandas typically live within a half mile (0.8 km) of flowing water such as rivers or streams.

(6) MONTHS		(8) MONTHS
‣ Ventures out of den with mother	‣ Nibbles bamboo, still nursing	‣ Fully weaned
‣ Climbs trees	‣ Weight: 42 pounds (19.1 kg)	‣ Full set of baby teeth
‣ Drinks water		‣ Eats only bamboo

 FEATURED FAMILY

This Is How It's Done

Bright sunshine is burning off the morning fog. The Qionglai giant panda cub is turning six months old today. He takes his first cautious steps outside the den, following his mother as she heads through the forest. At the edge of a stream, she lowers her head and begins lapping up water. The cub watches intently for a few moments. Then he dunks his face into the stream. Sputtering, he instantly draws back. Shaking his head, he snorts water from his nostrils. Then he tries again, this time gauging the distance right, and gets his first taste of fresh water.

24-HOUR DAY

10 HOURS ASLEEP

14 HOURS AWAKE

At eight to nine months old, a panda cub is fully weaned, which means it no longer needs its mother's milk. It still relies on its mother for protection from predators. To stay safe while its mother is eating, a cub may climb a tree. Adults rarely climb trees except to escape predators. A cub typically sleeps with its mother on the ground. Pandas sleep about 10 hours a day in increments of 2 to 4 hours. Cubs often fall from trees unharmed, but landing wrong can cause injury. Broken bones combined with predators, illness, and scarcity of food kill 40 percent of wild pandas within the first year of life.

---

1 YEAR

▸ Baby teeth fall out; permanent teeth grow in
▸ Weight: 88 pounds (39.9 kg)

2 YEARS

▸ Leaves mother to become independent
▸ Establishes home range
▸ Weight: 120 pounds (54.4 kg)

When a giant panda is two years old, it is about half the size it will be as a mature adult. Its mother has taught it how to select the best bamboo and how to find the safest branches for climbing and resting. Now is the time for the young panda to become independent. Its mother may have mated again. She turns her back on her offspring, signaling the young panda to leave her. The panda will not go far to establish its own home—usually near and sometimes even overlapping its mother's home range. Females' home ranges average 1.8 square miles (4.7 sq km), while male pandas' areas may be as large as 3.3 square miles (8.5 sq km). The young panda will continue to grow until, at age six or seven, it will be ready to find a mate.

CLOSE-UP
Scent marking

Pandas rub their hindquarters on trees and rocks to leave their scent. Females do this to tell males that they are ready to mate. Males do this to respond to females' messages. Their scent marks also tell other males to stay away from their chosen females.

FEATURED FAMILY

Practice Makes Perfect

At eight months old, the cub is now fully weaned. He has learned from his mother to select the slenderest bamboo stems. He reaches for a stem, and it moves in his paw! It is a stick insect bamboo mimic. Startled, the cub lets go. The insect scurries away. The mother chirps at the cub, encouraging him to climb a tree for a nap. Using his sharp claws, the cub pulls himself up to a high branch. Each time he climbs a tree, he gets a little better at it.

6 YEARS

- Full-grown
- Weight: 240 pounds (109 kg)
- Height, to the shoulder: 3 feet (0.9 m)
- Length: 6 feet (1.8 m)

7 YEARS

- Mates for the first time

20 YEARS

- End of life

CHAPTER FOUR
PANDA SPOTTING

In captivity, where veterinarians and zookeepers care for them, pandas can live into their 30s. But wild pandas seldom live more than 20 years. Research suggests that more than 10 percent of wild panda deaths are caused by infection and disease. About a quarter are caused by trauma—falling out of trees or being attacked by predators. But humans are the greatest threat to pandas' survival. Starvation—a direct result of habitat destruction—leads to one-third of all panda deaths. Because pandas eat mainly bamboo, the loss of their forests to agriculture, logging, and mining has been devastating to the wild giant panda population.

In an effort to help pandas, the Chinese government began to establish protected areas and research centers for pandas during the 1960s. Hunting them became illegal. But more needed to be done. In 1998, logging bans were put in place, further protecting many panda habitats. Yet the population continued to decline. Today, scientists from around the world have partnered with China to develop strategies to prevent pandas from disappearing from Earth forever. Captive-breeding programs have successfully brought hundreds of panda cubs into the world. In fact, since 1990, more pandas have been born in captivity than in the wild.

One of the top panda conservation facilities in the world is China's Chengdu Research Base of Panda Breeding. Founded in 1987 with 6 pandas, the center has grown to house more than 60 pandas today. More than 100 cubs have been born at Chengdu. Many of the young pandas are loaned to zoos around the world. There they mature and breed with pandas on loan from other places. This helps ensure genetic variety in panda family trees. Most captive-born pandas remain in captivity for their entire lives because they do not have the skills and knowledge to survive in the wild.

The wild panda population has slowly increased in recent years, thanks to China's attempts to curb the destruction of bamboo forests. However, not only do forests need to be saved, but destroyed forests need to be restored as well. This is the next stage in China's plan to protect its remaining wild pandas. Scientists agree that the only way to save the world's pandas is to provide them with safe and enduring places to live and reproduce in the wild.

"SINCE 1990, MORE PANDAS HAVE BEEN BORN IN CAPTIVITY THAN IN THE WILD."

FAMILY ALBUM
SNAPSHOTS

Dan-Dan was a female **Qinling panda** who lived at the Xi'an (*see-YIN*) QinLing Wildlife Park in Shaanxi Province, China, from 1985 to 2000.

The first **giant panda** kept outside China arrived at Chicago's Brookfield Zoo in 1936. She was named Su Lin (Young) after the first American woman to explore the Himalayas.

Pan Pan lived for 31 years and was part of a **giant panda** breeding program in Chengdu, China. He has more than 130 children, grandchildren, and great-grandchildren.

PAN PAN

Mei Sheng (*MAY sheng*) is a **giant panda** born at the San Diego Zoo in 2003. To aid in species recovery, he was sent to China's Wolong National Nature Reserve in 2007.

QIZAI

Qizai (*CHEEZ-eye*), a **Qinling panda**, was found abandoned at two months old. He has lived at the Shaanxi Foping National Nature Reserve in China since 2009.

Twins Jia Panpan (*tsee-YAH PAN-pan*) and Jia Yueyue (*tsee-YAH YEH-yeh*) were born in 2015 to **giant panda** parents at the Toronto Zoo. In 2018, the foursome moved to the Calgary Zoo for a five-year visit.

JIA PANPAN
JIA YUEYUE

In 2006, **giant panda** Mei Lan (*MAY lahn*) was born at Georgia's Atlanta Zoo. Thought to be female, Mei Lan was discovered to be male when he was moved to China in 2010.

Giant panda Tai Shan (*TIE shahn*) was born at Washington, D.C.'s National Zoo in 2005. He was featured in the Animal Planet documentary *Baby Panda's First Year* (2007).

Gu Gu (*GOO goo*) is a **giant panda** at Beijing Zoo who reminds us that pandas are wild animals. Three different times, zoo visitors who illegally entered his enclosure were bitten by Gu Gu.

Chi Chi (*CHEE chee*), a **giant panda** who lived at the London Zoo from 1958 to 1972, was the model for the World Wildlife Fund (WWF) logo, which was designed in 1961.

CHI CHI

Born at the San Diego Zoo in 1999, Hua Mei (*HWAH may*) is the first **giant panda** born in the U.S. to survive to adulthood. She now lives at China's Bifengxia (*bih-FEN-kuh-see-YAH*) Panda Base.

Xin Xin (*SEEN seen*), born in 1990, lives at Chapultepec Zoo in Mexico City. She is one of only a handful of **giant pandas** in North America outside the U.S.

Only two **giant pandas** are housed in the United Kingdom. Both live at the Edinburgh Zoo in Scotland.

WORDS to Know

captivity   living in a place from which escape is not possible

endangered   at risk of disappearing from the Earth forever

genetic   of or relating to genes (the basic physical units of heredity)

inbreeding   the breeding of individuals that are related to one another

mimic   an organism that imitates the appearance of another organism

mutation   a distinct change that may be passed on to future generations

nutrients   substances that give a living thing energy and help it grow

species   a group of living beings with shared characteristics and the ability to reproduce with one another

LEARN MORE

Books

Jazynka, Kitson, and Daniel Raven-Ellison. *Mission: Panda Rescue: All about Pandas and How to Save Them*. Washington, D.C.: National Geographic Kids, 2016.

Schreiber, Anne. *Pandas*. Washington, D.C.: National Geographic Kids, 2010.

Vitale, Ami. *Panda Love: Behind the Scenes at a Panda Sanctuary*. London: Hardie Grant Books, 2018.

Websites

"10 Facts about Pandas!" National Geographic Kids. https://www.natgeokids .com/nz/discover/animals/general-animals/ten-panda-facts/.

"Giant Panda." Smithsonian's National Zoo & Conservation Biology Institute. https://nationalzoo.si.edu/animals/giant-panda.

"Giant Panda." WWF. https://www.worldwildlife.org/species/giant-panda.

Documentaries

Brown, Nicolas. *Pandas: The Journey Home*. National Geographic Films, 2014.

Feldon, Amanda. *Pandamonium*. ITN Factual Productions, 2014.

Kobayashi, Tatsuhiko. *Pandas in the Wild*. Smithsonian Networks, 2012.

Note: Every effort has been made to ensure that any websites listed above were active at the time of publication. However, because of the nature of the Internet, it is impossible to guarantee that these sites will remain active indefinitely or that their contents will not be altered.

Visit

SAN DIEGO ZOO

Pandas at the zoo are also featured on a live Panda Cam on the zoo's website.

2920 Zoo Drive
San Diego, CA 92101

SMITHSONIAN'S NATIONAL ZOO & CONSERVATION BIOLOGY INSTITUTE

A leader in giant panda conservation with a successful breeding program.

3001 Connecticut Avenue NW
Washington, D.C. 20008

TORONTO ZOO

Home to the first two panda cubs ever born in Canada.

2000 Meadowvale Road
Toronto, ON
Canada M1B 5K7

ZOO ATLANTA

Animal Planet hosts a live Panda Cam on the zoo's website.

800 Cherokee Avenue SE
Atlanta, GA 30315

INDEX